EXPLORER TRAVEL GUIDES

SEAS

Nick Hunter

Raintree is an imprint of Capstone Global Library Limited, a company incorporated in England and Wales having its registered office at 7 Pilgrim Street, London, EC4V 6LB – Registered company number: 6695582

To contact Raintree, please phone 0845 6044371, fax + 44 (0) 1865 312263, or email myorders@raintreepublishers.co.uk.

Text © Capstone Global Library Limited 2014
First published in hardback in 2014
The moral rights of the proprietor have been asserted.

Edited by Adam Miller, Laura Knowles, and Claire Throp
Designed by Steve Mead
Original illustrations © Capstone Global Library Ltd 2014
Illustrated by H L Studios
Picture research by Tracy Cummins
Production by Victoria Fitzgerald
Originated by Capstone Global Library Ltd
Printed in China by China Translation and Printing Services

ISBN 978 1 406 26015 1
17 16 15 14 13
10 9 8 7 6 5 4 3 2 1

British Library Cataloguing in Publication Data
Hunter, Nick
Seas. – (Explorer travel guides)
910.9'162-dc23
A full catalogue record for this book is available from the British Library.

Acknowledgements
We would like to thank the following for permission to reproduce photographs: Corbis pp. 12 (© Francois Mousis/Sygma), 19 (© Bettmann), 37 (© Imaginechina/Corbis), 39 (© Song Zhenping/Xinhua Press); Getty Images pp. 9 (Central Press), 24 (Chad Ehlers); National Geographic Stock pp. 35 (© National Geographic/SuperStock), 36 (Alaska Stock Images); Newscom pp. 11 (Chinafotopress/Ding Qinglin), 15 (Henning Bagger/AFP/Getty Images); ORCA p. 26 (Tom Smoyer); Shutterstock pp. 4 (© Zacarias Pereira da Mata), 5 top, 6 (© Ramona Heim), 5 middle, 18 (© JonMilnes), 5 bottom, 29 (© Vlad61), 7 (© Lee Prince), 14 (© Michaela Stejskalova), 17 (© Georgios Kollidas), 21(© GagarinART), 25 (© Specta), 33 (©CyberEak); Superstock pp. 10 (© John Warburton Lee), 16 (© Science and Society), 30 (© Minden Pictures), 31 (© National Geographic); Alicia Hawkins-Roberts p. 32 (© Alicia Hawkins-Roberts).

Design elements: Shutterstock (© Stephan Kerkhofs), (© Nik Merkulov), (© vovan), (© SmileStudio), (© Petrov Stanislav Eduardovich), (© Nataliia Natykach), (© Phecsone).

Cover photograph of a reef scene with corals and fish, Komodo, Indonesia reproduced with permission of Superstock (© Stocktrek Images).

We would like to thank Daniel Block for his invaluable help in the preparation of this book.

Every effort has been made to contact copyright holders of material reproduced in this book. Any omissions will be rectified in subsequent printings if notice is given to the publisher.

CONTENTS

Some words are shown in bold, **like this**. You can find out what they mean by looking in the glossary.

Don't forget

These boxes will give you handy tips and remind you what to take on your sea adventures.

Amazing facts

Check out these boxes for amazing sea facts and figures.

Who's who

Find out more about sea experts and explorers of the past.

Conservation

Learn about conservation issues relating to seas.

ALL AT SEA

You are about to set sail on an expedition. On your travels, you will be surrounded by water stretching away on all sides as far as you can see. Sometimes these waters may be calm and beautiful; at other times, the water will be whipped up by storms into huge waves that could smash your ship to pieces on rocky coasts. Get ready to explore the world's oceans.

Storms at sea are one of the biggest dangers you'll face on your travels.

Amazing facts

Your journey will also take you to the pitch black of the deepest parts of the seabed, more than 10 kilometres (6 miles) below the surface.

The five oceans

Seas and oceans cover almost three-quarters of our planet. They are all linked together but we divide them into five oceans: the Pacific, Atlantic, Indian, Southern, and Arctic Oceans, as well as the seas and bays around the edge of these oceans.

Finding new lands across the ocean has fascinated people ever since they first began to explore. But the seas themselves also hold amazing secrets, such as beaches and cliffs and an amazing variety of living things. There's loads to explore, so where should you start?

Don't forget

You'll need a lot of equipment for your trip:

- Safety equipment, including a **liferaft** and lifejacket
- A **Global Positioning System (GPS)**, compass, and charts of the ocean so you know where you are and don't crash into a rock
- Plenty of food and drinking water. The sea is full of water but it's much too salty to drink.
- A sturdy boat and scientific instruments such as **sonar** for exploring the ocean.

Turn the page...

Find out about the different kinds of seas on pages 6–7.

Learn about exploring under the sea on pages 18–19.

Why is the lionfish so dangerous? Find out on page 29.

WHERE TO START

You may live close to the sea. Even if you live further away, you can always follow a river, as almost all rivers eventually flow to the sea. The world's seas and oceans are very varied, so you'll need to decide which kind of sea you want to explore.

Take a trip to the tropics

Tropical oceans are many people's favourite. They are found near the equator. These warm seas are teeming with life, especially around colourful **coral** reefs. Tropical seas are often dotted with beautiful islands, so you should make time to go diving or snorkelling.

In warm seas, you can find amazing tropical islands where you can relax after a hard day exploring.

Cold comfort

Colder seas are also fascinating in their own way. These are where you'll see majestic whales, the largest **mammals** on Earth. In the Arctic and Southern Oceans, you need to look out for giant icebergs, which can sink even the biggest ships.

Amazing facts

The Dead Sea between Israel and Jordan gets its name because it's the world's saltiest body of water. The Dead Sea is so salty that almost nothing can live in it.

The most dangerous part of an iceberg could be below the ocean's surface. You can only see the very tip of it sticking up above the water.

Conservation

Much of the Arctic Ocean is covered with thick ice, but things are changing. Earth's climate and oceans are getting warmer because of the gases humans release into the **atmosphere** from cars and industry. The area covered by ice is getting smaller all the time. This is bad news for animals such as polar bears.

Beneath the waves

The surface of the oceans is only the beginning. If you have the right equipment, you can discover a whole world beneath the waves. The deep ocean is divided into several zones, each of which has something different for the intrepid explorer.

Ocean zones

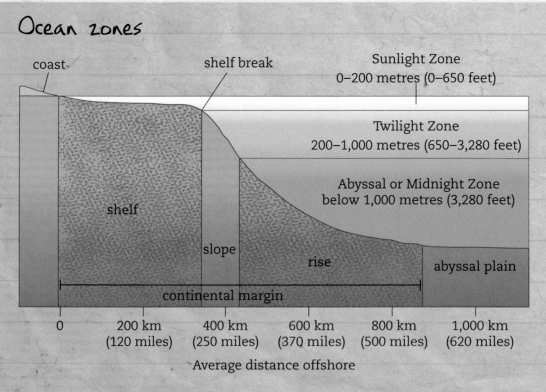

coast

shelf break

Sunlight Zone
0–200 metres (0–650 feet)

Twilight Zone
200–1,000 metres (650–3,280 feet)

Abyssal or Midnight Zone
below 1,000 metres (3,280 feet)

shelf

slope

rise

abyssal plain

continental margin

| 0 | 200 km (120 miles) | 400 km (250 miles) | 600 km (370 miles) | 800 km (500 miles) | 1,000 km (620 miles) |

Average distance offshore

Each layer of the ocean gets colder, darker, and more **inhospitable**.

Don't forget

Make sure you take the right equipment to explore beneath the waves:

- An **Aqua-Lung** enables you to breathe underwater.
- A **wetsuit**, mask, and flippers will help you to see and move more easily.
- In the deep ocean, you'll need a special armoured diving suit or submarine to protect you from the high **pressure**.

Ocean zones

The shallowest zone covers the first 200 metres (650 feet) below the surface. Sunlight reaches this zone so plants can grow. The seabed close to land is part of this zone. The next zone goes down to depths of around 1,000 metres (3,280 feet) and is often called the Twilight Zone. There is some light at the top, but at the bottom of this zone is total darkness. Below this is the abyss of very cold and dark water extending to the bottom of the ocean. Even here, you can find some living things.

Who's who

Auguste Piccard (1884–1962) designed his own **bathyscaphe**, which he used to explore the deep Atlantic Ocean. His son Jacques (1922–2008) went one better in 1960. He and American Don Walsh became the first people to descend 10,602 metres (34,783 feet) into the Mariana Trench in the Pacific Ocean, the deepest point in the world's oceans.

The *Trieste* was the submersible used to explore the Atlantic by Swiss scientist Auguste Piccard.

When to go

The seas and oceans of the world have many different conditions, just like the continents of the world. You have to think about weather conditions, ocean **currents**, and hazards such as ice when deciding the best time to explore.

Weather at sea is often hard to predict but there are some times to avoid. Oceans are normally at their coldest and roughest during the winter. Strong winds can cause huge waves that can damage even the biggest ships. The oceans and seas close to the **Polar** Regions are frozen during the winter months.

This ice-breaking ship is clearing a path through sea ice near Antarctica.

Hurricane season

Tropical seas are usually calmer but beware of **hurricanes** or **typhoons** if you're planning to travel in late summer or early autumn. These huge storms build up over tropical seas. They can be devastating to ships and coastal communities.

Amazing facts

If you see a waterspout, get away as fast as you can. These twisting funnels of water are caused by tornadoes over the ocean. They can pick up ships and anything else in their path.

Ocean currents circulate water around the oceans. They usually take warm water away from the tropics near the equator and bring colder water towards the equator. The Gulf Stream current carries warm water from the Gulf of Mexico to the Atlantic coasts of Europe, bringing warm, wet weather to western European countries.

WHO'S GOING WITH YOU?

You'll need a combination of ocean knowledge and bravery to have a successful expedition. Here are some of the best people in history to accompany you on your journey.

Expedition member: Ellen MacArthur (born 1976)

Ellen MacArthur became world famous in 2001 when she finished second in the Vendée-Globe solo around-the-world yacht race at the age of 24. She went on to break the world record for the fastest solo voyage around the world in 2005. MacArthur's bravery and skill will help you deal with any dangers that you'll face.

Potential job: Boat captain

Expedition member: Leif Eriksson (exploring around AD 1000)

Leif Eriksson led the first European expedition to North America, where he probably landed on the Newfoundland coast. He achieved all this in a Viking longship and **navigated** using the Sun and stars.

Potential job: Navigator

Expedition member: Robert Ballard (born 1942)

In 1985, Robert Ballard led the team that discovered the wreck of the *Titanic* deep beneath the Atlantic Ocean. He explored the wreck using the **submersible** vehicle *Alvin*.

Potential job: Underwater explorer

Expedition member: Joseph Banks (1743–1820)

Banks was still a young man when he accompanied Captain James Cook on his first voyage to the South Pacific. His enthusiasm and knowledge of plant and animal **species** would make him a great help on any expedition. Banks is also used to long voyages.

Potential job: Expedition naturalist

Expedition member: Ferdinand Magellan (1480–1521)

Don't take

Magellan led the first expedition to sail around the world, but he wasn't very lucky. He fell out with some of his captains and had them executed in South America. His crew suffered terribly from lack of food, and Magellan himself was killed by islanders in the Philippines.

EXPLORING SEAS AND OCEANS

When you go exploring, you'll be following a tradition that goes back to the first time that people went to sea in boats. The earliest known explorers were looking for people to trade with and new lands to conquer.

As sea-going trade grew, great port cities such as Venice in modern Italy grew up around the Mediterranean Sea.

 ## Who's who

Zheng He (1371–1433) was a Chinese admiral who explored the Indian Ocean as far as the coast of East Africa. His first expedition set out in 1405 with 300 ships and 28,000 people.

The first great sea explorers we know about were the Phoenicians. These trading people explored the Mediterranean Sea from their home in what is now Lebanon between 1000 and 500 BC. The Phoenicians were followed by the ancient Greeks, including the explorer Pytheas (c. 380–310 BC). His expedition ventured out of the Mediterranean and he probably discovered the British Isles.

Viking raiders

The greatest ocean explorers of ancient times were the Vikings. They developed navigation tools that enabled them to travel from the coasts of their native lands in northern Europe as far as North America.

Viking ships often had monsters carved on their bows (fronts) to strike fear into people as the raiders' ships approached new lands.

Amazing facts

The Vikings believed that the world was flat and surrounded by sea. This didn't stop them from exploring as far as they could.

The Age of Discovery

In the late 1400s, Europeans started to look beyond their coasts. Once again, their voyages were prompted by the search for wealth and power. Portuguese explorers started sailing down the west coast of Africa. They hoped to find a sea route to India that would replace the dangerous land route through Muslim lands, which could be hostile to Europeans. Vasco da Gama discovered this route in 1497.

This clock, invented by John Harrison in the 1750s, made accurate navigation at sea possible because it could keep correct time on a constantly moving boat.

Amazing facts

Food for ocean explorers was often disgusting, such as biscuits crawling with maggots. There was no refrigeration. Sailors often died from **scurvy**, until it was discovered that the disease could be cured by eating fruits such as limes, which we now know to be high in Vitamin C.

In 1492, Christopher Columbus, a young explorer from Genoa (which is now in Italy), had been funded by Spain for an ambitious voyage across the Atlantic Ocean towards what he thought was China. Instead, Columbus was the first European since Viking times to visit the Americas.

In the centuries that followed, Europeans set up trading routes and conquered **indigenous** peoples in the Americas, Asia, and Africa. Voyages like those of Captain Cook mapped the oceans, lands, and people they found.

Who's who

Captain James Cook (1728–1779) led three voyages of discovery for the British government. His first voyage explored the South Pacific Ocean, Australia, and New Zealand. Later voyages explored the Southern Ocean and tried to find a northern route between the Atlantic and Pacific Oceans. Although Cook was killed by Hawaiian islanders, his voyages were more peaceful and scientific than many who went before him.

Exploring the underwater world

By the 1900s, most of the world's oceans had been explored, but people knew little about what was beneath the surface. Early diving equipment was very heavy and uncomfortable and divers had to be linked to a surface ship to breathe underwater.

Don't forget

If you don't fancy diving, there are ways to explore underwater without getting wet:

- Sonar uses sound signals echoing off the seabed to map the shape of the undersea world.
- Robot submarines can be controlled from the surface to explore underwater and send back pictures and video.

There are more than 200 species of shark to look out for in the oceans. Most of them do not attack humans.

The first vehicles for exploring underwater were diving bells. These were open at the bottom. As long as they were upright, air pressure would stop water from filling the diving bell. By the 1930s, these had developed into the **bathysphere**, a hollow steel ball with two toughened windows designed to withstand extreme pressure in the deep ocean.

In the 1940s, the Aqua-Lung made it possible for ordinary divers to explore coral reefs and shipwrecks. Serious deep-ocean explorers developed submersibles that could travel into the deepest, darkest corners of the ocean.

Who's who

Jacques-Yves Cousteau (1910–1997) was prevented from becoming a pilot by an accident, so he turned his attention to exploring the underwater world. Cousteau's books and films of his expeditions introduced many people to the "silent world". He was the co-inventor of the Aqua-Lung, a tank of compressed air that divers could carry on their backs. He also helped develop Conshelf underwater stations, where "oceanauts" could live for days or weeks at a time.

SEEING THE SIGHTS

If you want to explore the world's oceans, you need to know what to look out for. Some of the most exciting features of seas are around the edges. The power of wind, waves, and other processes come together to help create dramatic coastlines all over the world.

Amazing facts

Sea cliffs are one of the most dramatic coastal features you will see on your journey. The world's highest sea cliffs are at Kalaupapa, Hawaii, in the Pacific Ocean. They are 1,010 metres (3,300 feet) high.

Exploring the coast

Some coastlines are likely to be very popular. Golden sandy beaches attract people who want to relax by the sea. Beaches are created when pebbles are laid down by the sea and gradually smashed into fine sand by crashing waves.

Other coastal landforms are more spectacular. Waves eat away, or erode, the rocks of coasts to create incredible rock stacks and arches. Be careful your boat doesn't end up wrecked on a rocky coast while you're admiring the view. Places like the rocky shores of South-west England have caused thousands of shipwrecks over the centuries.

Fjords, such as this one in Norway, are steep-sided valleys flooded by a rise in sea level.

Conservation

Coasts are always changing as the sea erodes rocks and sand and deposits them elsewhere on the coast. Although changing coasts are natural, they can be bad news for people because two in every five of the world's people live within 100 kilometres (60 miles) of the coast. Buildings and land can be gradually or suddenly swallowed up by the relentless sea.

Underwater landforms

Earth's surface is made up of interlocking plates of **crust**. Movements and changes in Earth's crust shape the oceans. You can see the effects of these changes as you explore, especially on the ocean floor. The seabed begins with the **continental shelf** at the edges of continents and then gets much deeper until you reach the **abyssal plains** of the deep ocean.

Amazing facts

Hydrothermal vents are found at the bottom of the Atlantic and Pacific Oceans. These vents in Earth's crust spew super-heated water onto the sea floor. The heat from the vents supports marine life such as clams and eyeless shrimp.

Undersea mountain ranges like the Mid-Atlantic Ridge can be found at the boundaries between sections of crust. These are the biggest mountain ranges in the world, but they're deep underwater. They are created by molten rock welling up from beneath the crust and hardening in the cold ocean.

Deep-sea trenches are found where one plate slides beneath another. These are the deepest parts of the ocean. You'll need the latest equipment to withstand the extreme pressure, darkness, and freezing temperatures of these dark depths.

Investigating islands

Make sure you have time to explore the islands produced by changes in Earth's crust. Some, like Iceland on the Mid-Atlantic Ridge, are undersea volcanoes that have reached the surface.

How island chains form

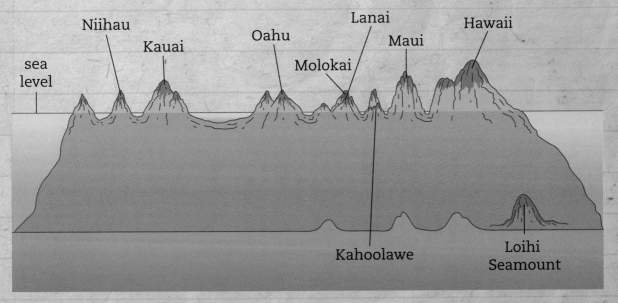

Some volcanic island chains, such as the Hawaiian islands, are caused by movements of Earth's crust across a hot spot that forces molten rock up to the surface.

 ## Don't forget

Tsunamis are huge, destructive waves caused by undersea earthquakes. In recent years, tsunamis have devastated coasts in the Indian and Pacific Oceans. If you are at sea when a tsunami strikes, head for deep water where the impact will be lower. If you hear a tsunami warning on land or feel the ground shake, head for high ground straight away. Tsunamis can pick up ships and destroy buildings.

Coral reefs

One of the greatest sights in the world's oceans is a coral reef. These reefs are actually made by tiny living things called coral polyps. Most of the hard reef is made from the skeletons of dead polyps. They are covered by a layer of living polyps.

Amazing facts

Coral reefs are not all the same. In the reefs around the Philippines, there are more than 400 different types of coral.

A coral atoll is a ring of coral around a central lagoon. The reef probably formed around an undersea volcano, which later disappeared beneath the waves.

You will find coral reefs in shallow tropical seas close to the edges of islands or continents. The biggest in the world is the Great Barrier Reef along the east coast of Australia. Coral reefs are incredibly important as they are home to around a quarter of the species of living things that live in the oceans. This also makes them fascinating and colourful places to dive and explore.

If you're exploring a coral reef, remember that these incredible places are made of fragile living things.

Conservation

Coral reefs need warm, clean water, and plenty of sunlight. **Pollution** and rising temperatures in the oceans are leading to coral bleaching, which damages the health of reefs. A survey of Australia's Great Barrier Reef in 2002 found that more than half of the areas tested showed signs of bleaching. Rising sea levels are another major threat to coral formations.

INTERVIEW WITH AN OCEAN EXPLORER

← Dr Edith Widder has been exploring the world's oceans for many years. In 2005, she founded the Ocean Research and Conservation Association (ORCA, www.teamorca.org) to protect and restore marine ecosystems.

Q: When did you first become interested in the oceans?

A: My love affair with the ocean began when I was 11 years old and I got to explore a coral reef in Fiji. I was enthralled with all the amazing life forms and I wanted to know more about them. In one of the tide pools, I found this exquisitely beautiful fish. I started to take it back to show my parents, but then I got worried that it might die so I carefully returned it to its home. It was a lucky thing because, if I had taken it, it might have hurt me far worse. It was years later before I learned that fish was a very poisonous lionfish. There's a moral in that story: be kind to life and life will be kind to you.

Q: Why is it important to explore the oceans?

A: The ocean is part of the vital life support system that **sustains** you as you hurtle through space on this tiny spaceship we call Earth. It provides the air you breathe and the food you eat and it contains untold wealth in as yet undiscovered **biomedical** compounds that could save your life or that of someone you love. There are great discoveries yet to be made in the ocean's depths, but we must learn to **nurture** and protect it or there will be nothing left to explore and nothing left to sustain us.

Q: What are the most important things you've learned?

A: I've learned that although the ocean seems vast and incredibly powerful, its ecosystems represent a delicate balance, which we need to understand, nurture, and protect. If people could understand that these life support systems are essential to sustain the fish and shrimp they want to eat, then perhaps we could work together to do a better job of protecting these habitats for future generations.

Q: Do you have any advice for ocean explorers?

A: To be an ocean explorer you must become an ocean protector.

OCEAN LIFE

There are thousands of different species of fish in the ocean, but you may also see the largest mammals on Earth and tiny **plankton**. During your expedition, make sure you have enough time to explore underwater life.

Don't forget

Some ocean life can be deadly to humans. Here are a few to avoid:

- Stonefish (Indian and Pacific Oceans): this venomous fish is especially dangerous because of its camouflage. Poisonous spines on its back contain enough poison to kill a human.
- Saltwater crocodile (shallow waters around Australia and Asian coasts): fast-moving, up to 6 metres (20 feet) long, with razor-sharp teeth and huge strength. Be very afraid!
- Box jellyfish (Australia and Asia): a sting from the tentacles of a "sea wasp" can kill a human being in just three minutes.

Whale watching

Whales are the biggest creatures in the ocean. The giant blue whale can be 30 metres (100 feet) long and weigh as much as 20 elephants. Many whales spend the winter in warmer seas and travel to cold polar oceans to feed in summer.

If you're lucky enough to see a whale, remember that these majestic creatures depend in many ways on other less glamorous living things, such as the krill and plankton that they eat.

The lionfish is beautiful but dangerous, with spines packed full of poison to protect it from predators.

Amazing facts

However far you travel around the oceans, you'll do well to beat the journey of a humpback whale. A single migrating whale was seen off the coast of Brazil and the coast of Madagascar, at least 9,800 kilometres (6,000 miles) away.

Creatures of the deep

Deep in the ocean, you will come across some of the most amazing living things on Earth. These creatures have to use some great tricks to survive. In many ways, they are as strange as any creatures dreamed up in science fiction.

The anglerfish uses a glowing lure to catch its prey.

In the deep ocean, there is no light to help animals find food. **Bioluminescent** animals make their own light from chemicals inside them. The lanternfish is one deep ocean fish that lights up to attract its **prey**. Food can be scarce in the deep ocean so deep-sea fish often have large mouths to catch whatever comes near them.

Deep-sea monster

Until recently, no human had ever captured or filmed a giant squid alive. These monsters can be more than 18 metres (60 feet) long. Their eyes alone are the size of dinner plates. These relatives of the octopus are said to have dragged sailors out of small boats, but there is still much that we don't know about them.

TRAVELGUIDES

Conservation

Many sea animals are under threat from pollution. Oil spills can cause environmental disasters when birds and other marine animals become covered in sticky oil. Unseen pollution also spreads across the oceans, when fertilizers and pesticides run off fields into rivers, which then carry them into the sea. Fumes from industry and vehicles are also absorbed by the oceans, making the water increasingly **acidic**. These and other sources of pollution could lead to many species of ocean life becoming **extinct** in coming years.

Birds and animals are poisoned by oil pollution as they try to remove it from their bodies. This pelican is having its feathers cleaned before being released back into the wild.

31

INTERVIEW WITH A MARINE BIOLOGIST

← Professor Callum Roberts is a marine biologist at the University of York in England. He came to love the sea growing up on the coast in Scotland's far north, where he spent endless hours walking the cliffs, letting his imagination fly with the birds to unknown shores, and plunge with the fish beneath green waves.

Q: When did you first become interested in problems facing the oceans?

A: At the age of 18, I made my first real dive on scuba and soon found myself exploring Saudi Arabia's magnificent coral reefs. Although the oceans had always seemed wild and beyond our influence, I soon realized that their life was easily damaged. It was the sight of my beloved coral reefs suffering from overfishing and pollution that made me dedicate my life to protecting the creatures of the sea.

Q: What are the biggest problems facing marine life?

A: The oceans of today are changing faster than at any time in human history, and humans are the cause. As well as catching fish faster than we should, the oceans are warming up, rising higher, and becoming more acidic, putting sea life under stress.

Q: What are the main changes you would make to protect the oceans?

A: These problems can still be solved. If we fished less, used less destructive methods to catch fish, wasted less, polluted less, and protected more places in marine parks, we could once again make the sea teem with life as it once did. The sea fascinates us: it can be beautiful and terrible, wondrous and serene, a road to riches or ruin. Ever since the dawn of humanity we have taken it for granted. But it needs our help now.

We need to start protecting the oceans before they become too damaged to save.

HUMAN-MADE MARVELS

As you travel the oceans, look out for signs of the generations of people who have explored before you. The first lighthouse, at Alexandria in Egypt, was built to guide ships more than 2,000 years ago. It was considered to be one of the wonders of the ancient world. Seas are also home to many modern wonders.

Conservation

Scientists are now trying to use the power of ocean winds and waves to generate electricity. Offshore wind turbines use the steady winds at sea to turn their sails. Wave power could generate even more power, but turbines need to be built that can withstand the huge force of storms at sea. This energy will be cleaner than burning fuels such as coal and oil, and it will never run out.

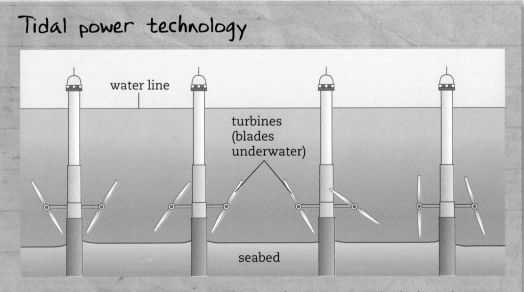

Tidal power technology

water line

turbines (blades underwater)

seabed

The movement of water pushes the blades of turbines around, which can be used to create energy.

Tunnels and bridges

People have always crossed the sea in boats, but new technology has created new connections. The United Kingdom and France, divided by the English Channel for several thousands of years, are now linked by the Channel Tunnel beneath the seabed. A combined tunnel and bridge now crosses the narrow Oresund Strait between Sweden and Denmark.

Stunning shipwrecks

Some of the most intriguing human-made wonders are the wrecks of ships that fell victim to storms, war, or even icebergs as they crossed the oceans. The most famous of these is the wreck of the *Titanic*, which hit an iceberg on her maiden voyage in 1912. However, the seabeds of the world are littered with millions of wrecks from centuries of seafaring – a warning to any explorer!

The wreck of the *Titanic* was discovered by ocean explorer Robert Ballard in 1985.

Living with the sea

Millions of people rely on the sea to live. You will probably meet some of them as you explore the oceans.

Those who go to sea to catch fish are some of the world's biggest experts on the oceans. Their lives often depend on their understanding of weather patterns and the dangers of the sea. Fishing methods range from large industrial ships to stilt fishing in the Indian Ocean. This is done by climbing up a pole in shallow water. From this perch, the fishers can see the fish without disturbing them.

Fishermen are experts in dealing with the sea at its worst.

 Amazing facts

Ocean waves are essential for one sport – surfing. In 2011, Garrett McNamara set a record for the biggest wave ever surfed when he rode an astonishing 24-metre- (79-foot-) high wave off the coast of Portugal.

Conservation

There are about 20 million fishing boats around the world. Most of these are small boats, but a few of them are huge industrial ships that account for 60 per cent of the fish caught from our seas. The **United Nations** says that people are catching too many fish. If this continues, they predict that the oceans will be almost empty of fish by 2050. One solution is to manage fishing so fish stocks are given time to recover and grow again after heavy fishing.

You will also meet people who earn their living from the sea in other ways. People love to spend their holidays by the sea, so people work to provide hotels, beautiful beaches, and boat trips for these holidays.

Rescue services risk their own lives at sea to help others.

ARE THE SEAS CHANGING?

Enjoy your time exploring the oceans because they could be very different in a few years' time. Seas are always changing as wind, waves, and other natural forces shape the world's coastlines. Sea animals also change over time to adapt to their environment.

But the world's seas are now going through greater change than ever before. Earth's climate is getting warmer because of the gases released into the atmosphere by human industry and transport. **Climate change** threatens to do major damage to ocean ecosystems as they struggle to deal with warmer waters. Pollution also threatens the health of many sea animals. At the same time, the huge quantities of fish we take from the sea are changing the balance of life in the oceans.

 Conservation

If climate change continues, it could lead to dramatic and dangerous changes. If the ice covering Greenland melts, the world's sea levels would rise by 7 metres (23 feet). Rising seas would flood many coastal areas that are home to millions of people.

Exploring and explaining

Explorers can help to investigate and explain the possible changes in our oceans. We need to make sure that our incredible oceans will still be around for future explorers.

Don't forget

Follow these rules to protect the oceans while you are exploring:

- Take all your rubbish home with you. A plastic bottle dropped in the ocean will stay there for around 250 years.
- Be careful not to damage fragile ecosystems such as coral reefs by treading on them or damaging them with boats.
- Respect marine life and do not take souvenirs.

This boat is powered by the Sun's energy through the solar panels that cover the top of its hull.

WORLD MAP OF OCEANS

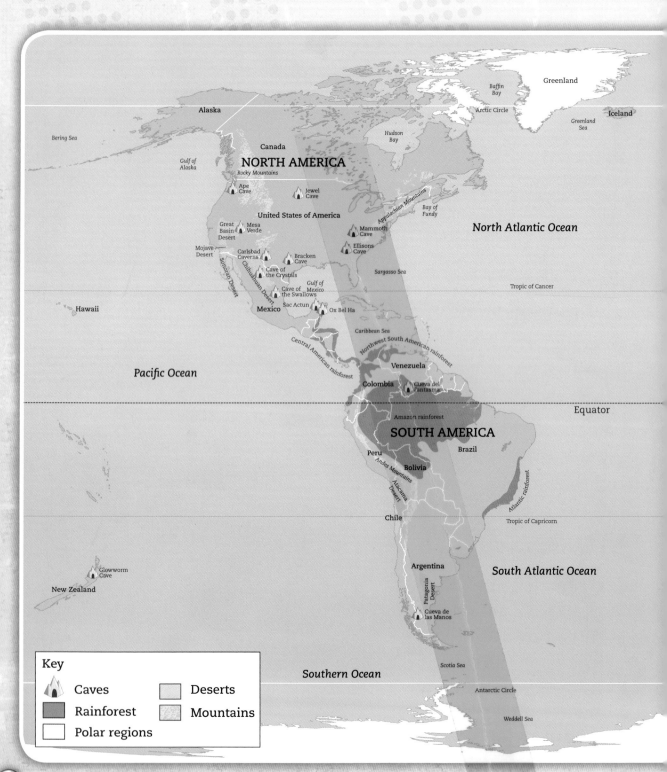

This map shows you where to find the world's oceans. There are many other exciting places to discover. Why not explore the mountains, caves, deserts, and rainforests shown on the map?

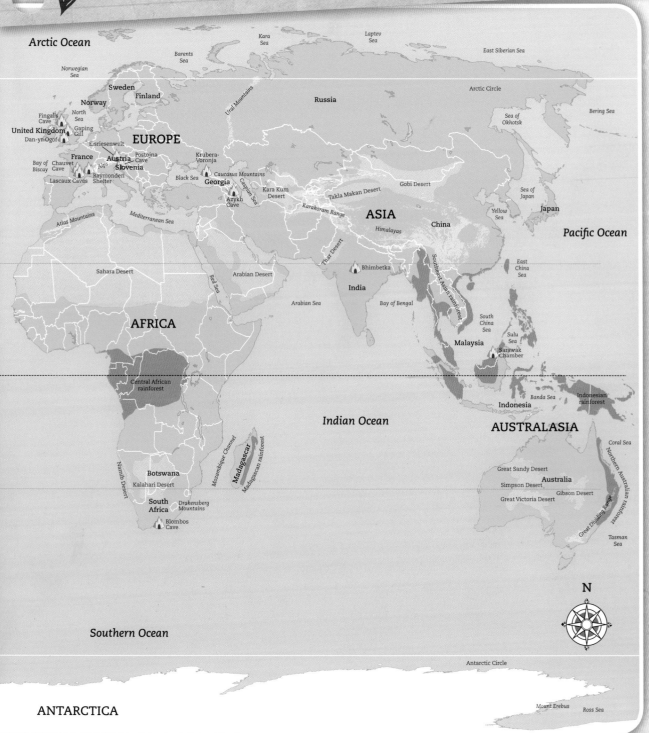

Arctic Ocean

Kara Sea

Laptev Sea

East Siberian Sea

Barents Sea

Norwegian Sea

Sweden

Finland

Norway

North Sea

Russia

Arctic Circle

Bering Sea

Sea of Okhotsk

Fingal's Cave

Gaping Gill

United Kingdom

Dan-yr-Ogof

EUROPE

Eisriesenwelt

Ural Mountains

France

Chauvet Cave

Austria

Alps

Slovenia

Postojna Cave

Krubera-Voronja

Bay of Biscay

Lascaux Caves

Raymonden Shelter

Black Sea

Caucasus Mountains

Georgia

Azykh Cave

Caspian Sea

Kara Kum Desert

Karakoram Range

Takla Makan Desert

Gobi Desert

Sea of Japan

Yellow Sea

Japan

Pacific Ocean

Atlas Mountains

Mediterranean Sea

Red Sea

Arabian Desert

Thar Desert

ASIA

Himalayas

China

Sahara Desert

Bhimbetka

India

Arabian Sea

Bay of Bengal

Southeast Asian rainforest

East China Sea

South China Sea

AFRICA

Malaysia

Sulu Sea

Sarawak Chamber

Central African rainforest

Banda Sea

Indonesia

Indonesian rainforest

Mozambique Channel

Madagascar

Madagascan rainforest

Indian Ocean

AUSTRALASIA

Coral Sea

Namib Desert

Botswana

Kalahari Desert

Great Sandy Desert

Simpson Desert

Australia

Gibson Desert

Northern Australian rainforest

South Africa

Drakensberg Mountains

Great Victoria Desert

Great Dividing Range

Tasman Sea

Blombos Cave

N

Southern Ocean

Antarctic Circle

ANTARCTICA

Mount Erebus

Ross Sea

TIMELINE

From 1000 BC	Phoenician traders explore the coasts of the Mediterranean Sea and North Africa
Around AD 1000	Leif Eriksson is the first European explorer to visit North America
1405	Zheng He of China leads the first of many expeditions in which he explores the Indian Ocean as far as Africa
1492	Christopher Columbus and his crew become the first Europeans since Leif Eriksson to cross the Atlantic Ocean to the Americas
1753	James Lind publishes a paper showing that citrus fruits, such as limes, could be used to treat and prevent scurvy
1768	James Cook captains the *Endeavour* on his first voyage round the world
1912	The liner *Titanic* hits an iceberg and sinks on her maiden voyage across the Atlantic Ocean, with the loss of more than 1,500 lives
1943	Jacques-Yves Cousteau uses an Aqua-Lung for the first time to explore beneath the ocean
1960	Jacques Piccard and Don Walsh are the first humans to reach the bottom of the Mariana Trench in the Pacific Ocean
1963	The new island of Surtsey appears in the Atlantic Ocean, caused by an undersea volcano
1985	Robert Ballard finds the wreck of the *Titanic* using the submersible craft *Alvin*
1994	The Channel Tunnel is completed beneath the sea between the United Kingdom and France
2004	A tsunami in the Indian Ocean causes devastation and the loss of more than 200,000 lives
2011	An undersea earthquake causes a massive tsunami to strike the coast of Japan, destroying coastal settlements and killing thousands of people

FACT FILE

THE WORLD'S OCEANS

Ocean	Size	Coastline	Lowest point	Ocean fact
Pacific	156 million square kilometres (60 million square miles)	135,663 kilometres (84,301 miles)	Challenger Deep in the Mariana Trench at −10,924 metres (−35,840 feet)	Almost equal in size to world's total land area
Atlantic	77 million square kilometres (30 million square miles)	111,866 kilometres (69,514 miles)	Milwaukee Deep in the Puerto Rico Trench at −8,605 metres (−28,232 feet)	Mid-Atlantic Ridge is a chain of mountains running down the middle of the ocean floor
Indian	69 million square kilometres (27 million square miles)	66,526 kilometres (41,339 miles)	Java Trench at −7,258 metres (−23,812 feet)	40 per cent of world's offshore oil production comes from the Indian Ocean
Southern	20 million square kilometres (7.7 million square miles)	17,968 kilometres (11,165 miles)	South Sandwich Trench at −7,235 metres (−23,737 feet)	Southern Ocean experiences the strongest winds of any ocean on Earth
Arctic	14 million square kilometres (5.4 million square miles)	45,389 kilometres (28,205 miles)	Fram Basin at −4,665 metres (−15,305 feet)	Almost totally ice-locked during winter months

- The average depth of the oceans is about 4 kilometres (2.5 miles).
- Around 99 per cent of all the space for living things on Earth is in the oceans. Humans have only explored about 10 per cent of this space.
- Australia's Great Barrier Reef is actually made up of around 3,000 separate reefs covering an area of 344,000 square kilometres (133,000 square miles). It is the world's largest living structure and can be seen from space.

GLOSSARY

abyssal plain deepest parts of the seabed, in the middle of the ocean

acidic acids are substances that can corrode materials and damage living things

Aqua-Lung tank containing compressed air that enables divers to breathe underwater

atmosphere layer of gases surrounding Earth, made of a mixture of gases that humans and living things need to breathe

bathyscaphe vehicle for exploring underwater, using a float to raise and lower itself

bathysphere metal sphere for exploring underwater, attached by a cable to a ship

bioluminescent describes a living thing able to create its own light using chemicals inside its body

biomedical relating to both biology and medicine

climate change gradual increase in temperature on Earth, mainly caused by human actions such as burning fossil fuels

continental shelf part of the seabed in relatively shallow water close to continents

coral type of simple animals with hard outer skeletons that come together to form reefs in tropical seas

crust outer layer of rock on Earth

current regular movement, such as the currents that move water around the oceans

ecosystem environment such as the ocean and the animals and plants that live in it

extinct no longer alive, particularly when referring to a species of animal that has totally died out

Global Positioning System (GPS) device that uses satellite signals to pinpoint the user's exact position

hurricane tropical storm with very strong swirling winds. In Asia, hurricanes are known as typhoons or cyclones.

hydrothermal vent crack in Earth's crust at the bottom of the ocean, through which super-heated water seeps into the ocean

indigenous people who originated in the place they now live

inhospitable not pleasant or comfortable

liferaft small inflatable boat for use in emergencies

mammal class of animals with a backbone in which mothers provide milk for their young, including humans, whales, and dolphins

navigate find your way, for example by using a compass or map

nurture provide food and other needs

plankton microscopic living things found in the ocean

polar relating to or close to North and South Poles

pollution damage done to air, water, or land because of material that has been released into it, usually by human activities, such as when oil spills into the sea

pressure force pressing on something, such as the high pressure created by water deep in the ocean

prey animal that is hunted by another animal for food

scurvy disease caused by lack of vitamin C, which particularly affected sailors until the end of the 1700s. Swollen and bleeding gums were a characteristic of the disease.

sonar system for finding objects under water by sending out sound pulses and measuring their return after they are reflected

species types of animal that all look similar and can breed together

submersible vehicle that operates underwater

sustain keep alive

tropical referring to the tropics, which is the area of Earth either side of the equator

tsunami huge, destructive wave caused by an undersea earthquake

typhoon name for a hurricane in the Pacific Ocean

United Nations organization of countries that aim to promote peace and cooperation

wetsuit suit worn by divers to keep them warm in cold waters

FIND OUT MORE

Books

Avoid Exploring with Captain Cook! (Danger Zone), Mark Bergin and David Antram (Book House, 2006)

Destroying the Oceans (Protecting Our Planet), Sarah Levete (Wayland 2012)

Great Explorers, Jim Pipe (OUP, 2008)

The World's Most Amazing Coasts (Landform Top Tens), Anna Claybourne (Raintree, 2010)

Tsunami Disasters (Catastrophe), John Hawkins (Franklin Watts, 2012)

Websites

www.bbc.co.uk/nature/habitats/Deep_sea

The BBC website has loads of great videos of the deep ocean.

www.cousteau.org

The website of the Cousteau Society includes details about the technology Jacques Cousteau used to explore beneath the oceans.

www.nhm.ac.uk/kids-only/life/life-sea/index.html

Learn more about life in the sea on the Natural History Museum's website.

Places to visit

National Maritime Museum

Romney Road

Greenwich

London SE10 9NF

www.rmg.co.uk

One of the largest collections of artefacts about the history of seafaring can be found at the National Maritime Museum.

There are many other maritime museums containing fascinating exhibits about the history of seafaring and ocean exploration. If you live near the sea, there may even be one in your town.

Marine national parks

Coral reefs such as Australia's Great Barrier Reef are just one of many marine national parks round the world. In the UK, the Pembrokeshire National Park is home to amazing cliffs, beaches, and other coastal landforms.

Further research

- Look in more detail at some of the great explorers introduced in this book. What did they discover and what were the motives and qualities that led them to explore? Did they do good or harm to the places they discovered?

- There is a huge variety of coastal landforms. Find out more about how the coastline changes over time.

- Ocean life faces many threats. Find out what those threats are and what you and your friends can do to help protect ocean ecosystems.

INDEX